CONFI

An Ex-SPY's Guide to Build Unwavering Confidence & Override Social Anxiety to Win in Any Situation

JAMES DAUGHERTY

© **Copyright 2016 - All rights reserved.**

The contents of this book may not be reproduced, duplicated or transmitted without direct written permission from the author. Under no circumstances will any legal responsibility or blame be held against the publisher for any reparation, damages, or monetary loss due to the information herein, either directly or indirectly.

Legal Notice:

This book is copyright protected. This is only for personal use. You cannot amend, distribute, sell, use, quote or paraphrase any part or the content within this book without the consent of the author.

Disclaimer Notice:

Please note the information contained within this document is for educational and entertainment purposes only. Every attempt has been made to provide accurate, up to date and reliable complete information. No warranties of any kind are expressed or implied. Readers acknowledge that the author is not engaging in the rendering of legal, financial, medical or professional advice. The content of this book has been derived from various sources. Please consult a licensed professional before attempting any techniques outlined in this book.

By reading this document, the reader agrees that under no circumstances are is the author responsible for any losses, direct or indirect, which are incurred as a result of the use of information contained within this document, including, but not limited to, —errors, omissions, or inaccuracies.

TABLE OF CONTENTS

Introduction 1

Part I: Basics for Developing Greater Confidence in Everyday Life 5

Chapter 1: Confidence: An Overview 6

Chapter 2: Basic Techniques for Developing Overall Self-Confidence 12

Chapter 3: Overcoming Limiting Beliefs........................ 29

Part 2: Preparing for Important Occasions- Dates, Interviews, Meetings and More 41

Chapter 4: Doing Your Homework 42

Chapter 5: Positive Visualization for Success 50

Chapter 6: Tips for the Day of the Event 56

Part3: Tricks to Override Social Anxiety in Stressful Situations 65

Chapter 7: The OODA Loop to Process and Respond to Surprising Situations................................ 66

Chapter 8: Additional Tactics for When Your Back is Against the Wall... 69

Conclusion 78

INTRODUCTION

Confidence. It is the one thing that separates the losers from the winners. And we are not talking sports; we are talking life.

Have you ever met someone that exudes confidence? Regardless of the challenge, they face it with a straight back, calm composure, and an "I can do it" attitude. Now, do you know what the difference between that person and you? That person KNOWS that they can do it and they have the skills to exude confidence. This person can be you too, as soon as you know the skills and techniques required for confidence. The good news is that this book can teach you just that.

My Back Story

You may be thinking, "Who is this guy that he is such an expert in confidence? Why should I listen to him?" Well, let me tell you. Here is what you need to know about me.

First, I want you to think about everything you have ever learned about spies from the movies. Think about action-packed scenes, careful surveillance, and anything else you have learned from Hollywood. Now, take these preconceived notions and toss them out the window. Real spy work is not action scenes and surveillance. Real spy work is usually done from afar; it's about getting things done with minimal fuss and without provocation. It's quiet and unassuming data gathering for the most part. Although sometimes you find yourself in real, dangerous situations with life-death consequences.

You'd also be surprised to find that spy work isn't necessarily gadgets and gizmos that do your work for you. Most of the time, it comes down to human psychological skills and the ability to improvise in any situation. And these skills can be developed and learned with a little practice.

I have to skip over some of the more specific details, as almost everything I have done over the past two decades is classified. What you need to know is that I am an Ex-CIA spy and that I have spent plenty of time in the field, improvising in situations where shakiness or a lack of confidence could cause death. Real names will be omitted as I detail some of my jobs and experiences around the world for the same reason.

I got my start in 1994 working a desk job for the FBI in my home state of Virginia. About a decade into my stint with them, my parents died in a car accident in our home town whilst sliding on an icy road into oncoming traffic one winter. Since it was my ties to my family that had kept me at home all these years, I decided to become a field agent as I figured I'd get to see a fair deal more than

CONFIDENCE

I currently was paper pushing behind a desk in Richmond. The transition wasn't as smooth as I'd anticipated. But a little under nine months after undertaking the training, I was a fully fledged Special Agent in the FBI. It took me all across the country, initially shadowing more experienced agents on white collar fraud cases but I soon graduated onto much more interesting work.

I have to confess that I did not know how good I would be at first. Everything that I had done in life up to this point though, I had succeeded at. From top grades in high school to the football scholarship at Florida State that I used to study forensics and psychology, I had succeeded in pretty much everything I'd tried. Regardless of why, I was good.

The FBI took note of this as they put me on more dangerous assignments as an undercover agent. I infiltrated criminal organizations and helped to take down illegal rackets of all descriptions. Sex, drugs, you name it. Eventually, I ended up on a case with another agent, an American spy. It was through him that I met my latest employer.

So, why am I an expert in confidence? I have since left the CIA, but after many years working for them as a spy I had acquired a number unique skill sets, counterintelligence, hand-to-hand combat, lock picking, body language analysis just to name a few. However there is one overriding factor that underpins them all, self-confidence. You need it in every cell of your body to perform all of the above tasks efficiently and under duress. It's not a luxury, it's a necessity. Leaders of top crime organizations are very cautious when it comes to trust. Giving off even the slightest nervous gesture at the wrong time can cost you your life. As someone with a psychology background and who has plenty of career experience with confidence, it is my belief that there is no one better to teach you.

Now that you know my qualifications and what I bring to the table, let's dive in. The following chapters will teach you everything that you need to exude confidence, even in life or death situations. Don't worry, I will provide plenty of stories about my work in the field (as well as real life examples that could apply to you) along the way to keep things interesting. But ultimately provide you with the tools and knowledge on how to be confident and excel in any situation.

PART I

BASICS FOR DEVELOPING GREATER CONFIDENCE IN EVERYDAY LIFE

CHAPTER 1

CONFIDENCE: AN OVERVIEW

Before we can begin to delve into confidence and the techniques that can help you succeed in things you never before imagined, it is important to develop an understanding of what it truly is. Confidence can be defined a few different ways. For the purpose of this book, you should view confidence as a feeling of trust and self-assurance in yourself. It is the belief that you will succeed in all that you do and the ability to follow through with the right actions and attitude to make what you want happen.

True confidence and self-efficacy in any area of life, isn't something that can be turned on by a switch. It's actually something that is cultivated over time.

> Confidence comes from competence, full stop.

I will concentrate on the techniques which will allow you to do this in part 1 of this book. Part 2 and part 3 are where I'll highlight the tips & tricks to attain greater confidence in situational settings (business meetings, interviews & social dates) as well as overriding social anxiety when your back is against the wall. This is usually viewed as the 'sexy' stuff people are itching to get to. The spy tips for getting out of dodge. However, I can assure you. Part one is where you want to spend most of your time. Ensuring you develop the long term self-confidence traits that will have the biggest pay-off and knock-on effect to every area of your life in the long run.

How Confidence Helps You Succeed

Do you know what all of the most successful people have in common? From the leading executives of companies to A-list celebrities, successful people know their abilities and they act on them.

My first encounter with an exuberantly confident person occurred shortly after my parents' passing. It was at this time that I was first gaining interest in work beyond a desk job. Now, you should know that my department did not let just anyone go into the field. I was fortunate enough to observe one of my coworkers (another desk agent) that told the boss he was ready to move on and try his luck in the field.

As my coworker (let's call him Rick) interacted with our senior officer, he stood straight. His voice was unwavering as he told him, "I'm just ready. I understand the dangers of the job. Not only do I understand them, I fully anticipate the possible dangers and I am prepared to deal with them." While our boss told Rick he would have to undergo some extra training and take a few tests before he would be able to be considered for a field position, Rick did it. He convinced the guy to give him the shot to try it, simply by projecting his own confidence in the position. I have to confess that it was very similar to the technique I would use about 2 months later when I had decided I was ready to move on in my career.

So, how exactly can greater confidence help you exceed in life? Here are just a handful of reasons.

#1: Confident People Stand Up for Themselves (take no sh*t)

Something else that I should tell you is that I had been a quiet, reserved person for years before my parents passed away. Being a psychology minor, I already knew all of the techniques that can be used to develop confidence. I had never really put them to the test, because I was a hard worker committed to my desk job. You may find this strange coming from an Ex-CIA field operative, but some of the toughest and highly skilled people I met whilst in the agency were the quietest.

One thing I noticed was that after time, people would start to try to push their work off on me. Since I didn't have a family and didn't have much of a social life, they assumed that I had time to work weekends and complete unfinished tasks. It was during this time that I started to stand up for myself. After all, just because I lived a quiet life I shouldn't have to complete other people's work.

The major benefit of having confidence strong enough to stand up for yourself is that you can demand respect for yourself. When my coworkers were trying to push work on me, they were using me. This was an injustice, especially as it happened more and more frequently. You may find that you encounter other injustices in your life as well. You may find that your spouse's parent hates you for no reason or that you get passed up for a promotion because the other person is chummy with your boss. Having confidence allows you to speak out against situations like these and demand respect for yourself, without being mean or aggressive. I'm not saying do not be helpful to others when you can, but often having the confidence to say 'no' can be one of the most liberating things you can do.

#2: Confident People Easily Overcome Their Fears

Have you ever let fear hold you back? Maybe you missed out on a promotion at work because you didn't speak up about your ideas or maybe you didn't go to a fun party because you were afraid you would feel uncomfortable. When you are truly self-confident, you do not have to worry about missed opportunities because you are willing to give anything your best shot. You do not let fears such as what others will think of you or whether you will succeed or fail get in your way.

#3: Confident People Believe they Exceed, and Excel

When you have a higher level of self-confidence, you will find that you set the bar high for yourself in terms of your expectations. When you set these expectations for yourself, the confident person doesn't let anything hold them back. They reach their expectations and go even farther, always testing their limits to become the best that they can be. When you are confident, you will find that you can excel at anything as long as you keep your faith in yourself. Life begins at the edge of your comfort zone as they say. True self-confidence allows you to push the boundaries of this place and deal with the discomfort much more easily. Then the magic happens.

#4: Confident People Don't Let Anyone or Anything Hold Them Back

Have you ever had the feeling that you weren't good enough and passed up a promotion or chance to lead? Or have you ever had an idea that you did not share or follow through on because you were worried about what other people would think? When you have self-confidence, nothing will hold you back. You will be able to share ideas and eagerly jump on new opportunities because you believe you can achieve anything.

Confidence and Your Interactions with Other People

If you have ever worked closely with someone who is truly self-confident, then you already know how this projects a certain air about a person. It means that you can do what you choose, whether you adhere to someone's requests or say no so you can focus on your own work.

CONFIDENCE

Much like you notice the confidence of others, other people can sense it you also. People will approach you with bigger, better opportunities because they know that you can not only handle the tasks in front of you, but that you will excel at them. When you are confident, you have the capability of saying yes to requests that present you with opportunities, though you will find that you can also say no. When you say no, your air of confidence will keep people from pestering you, because they realize that you have your own commitments to attend to. Overall, when you are confident, you will find that your interactions with other significantly improve.

Now that you have an understanding of what real confidence is, I want you to stop for a moment and reflect on your life. Consider any possible opportunities that you missed, any injustices that you have let carry on, and any goals that you did not try to achieve because you were afraid to fail. Now, imagine how different your life would be if you were confident enough that none of these things existed. It is too late to change the past, but it is not too late to start moving towards confidence today to build a better, more fulfilling future.

CHAPTER 2

BASIC TECHNIQUES FOR DEVELOPING OVERALL SELF-CONFIDENCE

The first thing that you should know is regardless of your background, your current level of confidence or how introverted you consider yourself, you can develop your confidence with the proper mindset and tools. With the right techniques, anyone can develop it. The tips within the following chapter will teach you the basics for developing unwavering self-confidence for your day to day life.

#1: Attitude Is Everything

In my time with the CIA, I once had to work with a woman we will call Barbara. Her looks and outgoing personality had gotten her far undercover and she was working close to one of New York's most prominent Mafia bosses. It was probably her cocky attitude that had gotten Barbara so close in the first place, they seemed almost intimidated by a powerful woman who could speak her mind. Unfortunately, it also proved to be her downfall. Barbara was so sure of herself that she became complacent.

It took months to infiltrate this particular mafia family and only moments to destroy it when Barbara forgot a detail of her back story. We got her out alive but her entire cover had been blown. Undoubtedly criminal undercover work is acutely stressful and difficult to manage, and single moments of hubris or unprofessionalism can undue months of careful work.

Do you know what Barbara's major mistake was? She was too sure of herself. There is such a thing as being too confident, even the best of us have limitations. As you develop your self-confidence, remember not to be arrogant or cocky. Being too sure of yourself can make you feel as if you do not need to continue practicing the things that got you to where you are in the first place.

To prevent yourself from giving off a better-than-you attitude, remember to stay humble. It is okay to be assertive, but you should also strive to be empathetic. You should be humble in the way that you realize that learning is a never-ending process. Do not be afraid to take in more data and information or to learn more about a subject you are an expert in. Allow this humbleness to become an elegant personality trait to compliment your newfound assertiveness.

#2: Build Your Confidence Slowly and Learn from Your Mistakes

You cannot expect yourself to wake up tomorrow and just be confident if deep down you are not. It's not like toasting some bread which you can do regardless of how you feel. Confidence is a learning process and is something that requires continual work and competence in several areas. One of the key to self-confidence and success is to make your mistakes early on, when the stakes are not so high. When you do fail, look at the situation from a critical point of view and see where you went wrong. When you learn what your mistakes were, evaluate them and what you could have done differently so that you do not make the same one twice. Excel by learning, that is the true way to be excellent.

In my early days as an FBI field agent, I found myself in a tight situation. My partner and I were working on a drug bust, dealing with mid-level guys in the basement of a Chicago liquor store. We had three objectives. Get in. Buy the evidence. Get out. The guys would be arrested later, after we were moved to safety and our cover was secured. The trouble started when one of the guys began asking too many questions regarding our distribution connections. There were two of them and one of them had taken my partner into another room to check the product. I have to confess that I was mostly following his lead before this moment. Unfortunately, my first test on my own didn't go according to plan.

The guy I was dealing with became increasingly fidgety as if he was readying himself something. He was, to rob us. I should have been able to talk him out of it, to persuade him otherwise. But I choked. The only thing that saved us was the fact that we were dealing with mid-level guys who were sloppy and neither was armed. I yelled at my partner as I took my guy down, the second he sprinted toward a bookshelf where I assumed he had a gun hidden. This would prove to be right after later inspection of the room. They were both in handcuffs within a minute, but our cover was blown.

I definitely learned the importance of being able to take lead in the moment. I learned not to depend on my partner so much and that I needed to come fresh and prepared to work every day. Even the slightest stutter on my part could cost us a case, or our lives.

#3: Create a Positive Feedback Loop

Have you ever heard that confidence is an ingrained trait, that you are either confident or you are not? This misconception could not be further from the truth. Confidence is a trait that can be learned. Critics of this say that you cannot simply change the way you think. While this is true to some degree, you can certainly change your actions. One of the best ways to build confidence is to increase your self-esteem by creating a positive feedback loop.

Basically, a positive feedback loop is successes and the feelings that go along with them. It is small victories and achievements that will build your overall confidence. It is surprisingly easy to create a positive feedback loop. All you have to do is set small goals for yourself. As you achieve, you increase the size of your goals. Each time that you complete a goal, it builds your confidence. In this way, your actions can dictate the way that you think and eventually lead you to feel more confident in yourself.

I want you to take a moment to imagine a scenario; one that likely affects you if you struggle with self-confidence. Imagine that you have to give a speech in front of a room full of people. Frightening, right? The thought of being in front of all those people and the risk of stumbling over your words or even freezing up and not being able to talk at all. The good news is that I don't recommend you get on stage in a room full of people to try this out, not just yet.

The easiest way to get over the lack of confidence in this situation, as well as any other, is to take small steps until you are confident enough to attempt climbing on stage. Start by giving a presentation in front of just two people, even if they are only friends. Move on to a small room and then maybe a small stage. Eventually, you will build the competence in speaking in front of people so much so that you could speak in front of a gala or give a presentation in a room full of executives. Confidence to do so will just come as a by-product of the above practice and steps.

As a spy, confidence is always required, whether I am negotiating with a small group of terrorists or impersonating a high level art dealer. You end up in many compromising situations which look to an outsider as if you've been thrown in at the deep end. The truth is that there had been many smaller, less important experiences of a similar nature beforehand to prepare for this one. When you create these positive feedback loops you become confident enough to act your way out of even the most intense situations and are successful more often than not. For me it was a matter of life and death on occasions. Although speaking in front of a crowd may seem like that for you, I can assure you with the right practice it is not!

#4: Stack Your Skills to Aggregate Confidence

Have you ever tried something and failed, losing some confidence in the process? The natural reaction to failure is an unwillingness to try. This bad habit, however, is one that takes a toll on your overall confidence over time. As you fail at different things, you become less inclined to try new things. The downfall of this mental scarring from failures both big and small is a shut out of the chance of further progression. You are discouraged to try new things, leading you to hide in your comfort zone and hold yourself back from success.

Confidence requires you to step outside of your comfort zone. You must try new things and try to develop new skills. As you find yourself becoming more comfortable and learning new skills, you will naturally become more confident. The more skills that you aggregate, the more self-confidence you will possess. Building small skills over time and on top of one another has an exponential/compounding effect on confidence as the sum of two related skills equals more than 2. Try making those small wins everyday that have a big effect over time.

#5: Play to Your Strengths

Even the most talented people are likely to have at least one area that they struggle with. Being confident is about owning the fact that you are not perfect just as much as it is about having self-confidence in your strengths. When you interact with others, showcase your strengths and downplay your weaknesses. Remember, being confident in your abilities does not mean that you will suddenly be successful at something you once struggled with and it is okay to have areas you do not excel in.

Something else you would do well to remember is that not everything has to be perfect. In fact, you are always going to be your biggest critic of the work you produce so even when we do not see something as flawless, others will think we did a great job. You can overcome this by trying to be 70-80% satisfied with the critical work you do. The significant stuff that will make the most impact on your success. In almost all cases, this will be satisfactory in the eyes of others because they are not going to pick apart your work and look for flaws. But it's not about fooling people; it's about being efficient with your time and moving onto the next thing as soon as the previous task is working and operationally up to scratch. You can always go and revise it at a later date. Again, it's all about skill stacking.

#6: Accept What You Cannot Change

Regardless of your level of confidence, there are still fixed occurrences and interactions in life that you cannot change. This could include the death of a friend or family member, a car accident or other incident that you do not have any control over, or a mistake that you have already made. In all of these situations and many others, the incident already happened and it cannot be changed. The only thing that you can do, therefore, is accept what has happened.

If you find yourself dwelling on the occurrence, set a timer. Think about the situation for three minutes. In this time, think about your future actions and if there is anything you can do that may change the situation. In some cases, you may find that an apology is due to someone. In others, such as a car accident, you can take the steps to ensure future transportation where you need it and contact your insurance company. Dwelling on the past, however, fixes nothing. Regardless of the situation you are facing, if you cannot change it, then you must simply accept what has happened. Learn from your mistakes if there were any and continue to take steps for the future instead of dwelling on things you cannot change.

Return to the story that I told you about my first big mistake, when I blew my cover and my partner's cover during a drug bust. After the incident, it was hard not to beat myself up over it. It had already happened though and there was no way to go back and change it.

Do you know what I did? Well, in the moment I did not have time to dwell on my mistake. It took me a split second to know what I had to do, take down the suspect and protect the safety of my partner.

I followed my own advice after the fact. I allowed myself three minutes to think about the situation and what I would do. I considered what happened and decided the best approach was to think about my mistakes in the situation, and learn from them. Then, I approached my boss to talk about the issue and told him I learned my mistakes. He was glad I took the initiative and instead of being thrown back on desk jobs, he decided to give me another chance.

Remember, in cases where it seems like you have no control, surrender to the situation which actually allows you to have control over it. Accept what you cannot change and then control it, by refusing it to cause you any further distress in your life.

#7: Excessive Positive Thinking is NOT the Answer

Have you ever met one of those people who are always chipper (and possibly annoying), regardless of what life throws at them? While this can be a good trait to have to an extent, too much positivity leads you to live a sheltered life. You will not be able to learn from your mistakes, nor will you be able to respond appropriately to stressful situations. You should note that positivity in general is not the same as positive visualization, a technique that you will learn later which can be quite effective for helping you develop confidence in situational settings.

You will not experience change from constantly badgering yourself with motivational quotes and videos. These things will give you a momentary motivational shot in the arm, but ultimately will fail you as excessive positive thinking is hard work. You need inspiration not motivation for the bigger things you are trying to achieve. Then you will just get on with them regardless of your current emotional state. This is the true path of least resistance to a confident and ultimately successful life.

The key is learning how to remove the negative thinking from your life, including irrational worrying and self-doubt. Have you ever spent hours worrying about something that never happened? This is because 99% of what people worry about NEVER happens. Will I lose my job? Will my girlfriend cheat on me? Will I have enough money to pay the bills this month?

The truly stressful situations that you will inevitably encounter will be curve balls you won't see coming and that are almost impossible to fully anticipate or prepare for. Such as a climbing accident, market crash or a sudden loss of a family member. However, you should remember that it is okay if things blind side you, because you are always able to deal with them at the time. Think of all of the situations you have handled successfully in the past. You have done it before (as you are still here to tell the tale) and you will do it again in the future. You should take great comfort in this, and don't worry, you will learn some tips later on in this book that will help prepare you and give you an even greater edge for when these sudden situations do arise.

#8: Consistency and Good Habits Are Key

Consider your current daily routine. Is it consistent or do you judge whether or not you workout by how you feel in the morning? How good are your eating habits? Do you find yourself worn out after a day of eating junk food? Something I have found to be true myself is that consistent habits really do make the difference. If you come from a military background or just had a strict family upbringing, you will naturally do this.

When you exercise regularly, wake up early and eat a clean, healthy diet regularly, it really does have a positive impact on the way that you feel and function. The science behind this one is pretty simply. Regular movement (especially longer distance cardiovascular exercise) and better fuel both produce higher levels of the 'feel good' neurotransmitters dopamine and serotonin within the brain. This will give you a sense of overall well being and help with everything from mood to memory. A lot of confidence in yourself can be derived from doing just this.

I can attest myself that regular exercise and a clean eating routine makes all the difference in the way that I feel throughout the day. As a spy, I had to remain sharp as a tack. Even the slightest mental fogginess or slow reflexes could have cost me my life and put others in danger. This is the reason that I get up at least two hours before work each morning. I exercise, shower, and then eat a healthy breakfast that provides me the nutrition that my brain and body needs throughout the day. While you do not have to follow my specific routine, you should find one that works for you, and stick to it! You will notice significant changes in the way that you feel within a week.

#9: Look the Part, Play the Part, Feel the Part

Have you ever done something or been exposed to something, to later have it ingrained as a part of your personality? Think about the way that living in a certain area can cause you to develop an accent. Confidence works much in the same way, because after doing something deliberately for a long period of time, will force it to become part of your body's physiology and mental makeup.

When you are trying to be confident, you must act that way. While you will not necessarily start to feel confident right away, the theory is that over time confidence will become part of your physiology. As you go about your day, try standing tall and acting confident. Speak clearly and boldly as you state your thoughts. Make your movements sure. Eventually, after taking these actions in a confident manner, you will just appear more confident to others. Pretty quickly, this will start to feed into the inner confidence further supporting the feedback loops.

I remember one time I was working undercover as an air conditioning contractor, trying to gather intel on a prostitution ring that was being run out of a inner city warehouse. My job was simple. Once again, in and out but complete my objective. At this time, I would be placing microphones and video feeds that would allow us to complete surveillance on this organization.

The guys had a pretty regular schedule. As my luck has it, they switched things up and showed up for one of their meetings while I was surveying the buildings air ducts. Of course they took notice of me, but my quick, on-the-spot thinking helped me remain in character and congruent with my cover story. This was the first time that I had been confronted on a mission since the incident in the Chicago liquor store and honestly the first time my boss had let me work in the field for a couple months. This time was different though. I had been working on my cover stories and speech patterns in my time off whilst doing minor surveillance and other rookie work. I stood straighter and I thought more clearly and spoke with a newfound confidence and self assurance. I answered all of their probing and menial questions flawlessly and carried along on my way with these chaps being none the wiser my surveillance work was about to bring them down.

#10: Start Your Day with Affirmations

This one may seem strange coming from an Ex-FBI and CIA intelligence field operative. But it is actually something we practiced often when prepping for operations to instill critical operational and behavioral characteristics of any particular undercover personality trait. For us it was a matter of ingraining attributes so deep into the subconscious mind that they would hold up under extreme duress. But the same can be applied very successfully in everyday life.

An affirmation is essentially a form of auto suggestion in which a statement of a desirable outcome or condition is deliberately meditated on or repeated in the mind and out loud to bring about its existence in the 'real world'.

The science behind why affirmation practices seem to work and yield positive results in subjects that consistently use them isn't always clear. It certainly produces some rewiring of the brain synapse neurochemistry on some level. Studies have demonstrated that participants who were reciting affirmed statements (compared with un-affirmed participants) showed increased activity in key regions of the brain's self-processing (medial pre-frontal cortex) and valuation (ventral striatum) systems when reflecting on future-oriented core values.

This may be a deeper discussion for future exploration. I plan to write a book in the coming months on exactly what positive habits one should undertake on a daily basis that will go into much more scientific detail on the subject. But for now, let's say positive affirmations certainly work and that you should incorporate them to some extent in your daily routines to improve overall confidence. So here is some practical advice on it.

I want you to think for a moment about something that you are sensitive about. It could be one of your physical features like a large nose or being overweight, or a characteristic like feeling as if you are not smart enough or fast enough. Now that you are thinking of that, I want you to think back to when you first developed this belief. Did you wake up one morning and think, "my nose is too big" or did somebody comment or make a joke about your nose? Regardless of whether it was you or someone else that first stated this, there are good chances that you did not believe it right away. You thought it over time or you were told it over time. Eventually, you started to believe it and it became a weakness in your eyes.

In the same way that negative thoughts weasel their way into your mind and become imbedded with time, you will find that positive thoughts do the same. While this will not be an instant change that happens overnight, you will find that starting your day with positive affirmations will help build self-confidence over time, especially if they are related to a specific area you have trouble with.

Have you ever been complimented by someone who told you that you were intelligent or beautiful or handsome? Chances are that you caught yourself smiling later in the day thinking about how great it is that someone thinks that way of you. You may have even caught yourself looking in the mirror, thinking, "Maybe I really am attractive". Positive affirmations have this effect over time, but you do not have to wait for a compliment from someone else to achieve it.

How-to Guide for Positive Affirmations for Confidence

The best time to do your positive affirmations is in the morning, possibly as you brush your teeth since the best way to practice affirmations is in front of a mirror. I keep my affirmations taped alongside my bathroom mirror, since it is a regular reminder when I am freshening up in the morning. Look yourself in the eyes and say each affirmation. Say it confidently and clearly, allowing its message to sink into your mind. You will want to say each affirmation a few times before moving on to the next.

You can choose the affirmations that work best for you, but here is a look at my personal list to help me maintain my confidence, both in my work as a spy and in my everyday life.

1. I trust myself completely and approve of my traits and my actions.

2. Meeting strangers is second nature to me and I approach them with enthusiasm.

3. I am confident in my ideas and will speak clearly when I present them.

4. I do not stress about the past, I live presently and feel confident of my future.

5. I solve problems by focusing on finding the solution. I am confident I know the best solution.

6. I emanate confidence in all of my daily interactions.

7. People respect my ideas and me because I am sure of myself.

8. I am healthy and clean. My inner well being is matched by my outer confidence.

9. I adapt to change well and am confident enough to handle new situations.

10. I am confident enough to rely on myself in any situation.

You can adjust what you say to match your own personal struggles, but this is the list that works best for me. If you do create your own affirmations, make them bold, positive statements that will instill confidence in you.

As you read over these techniques, try not to become overwhelmed. While you can easily finish reading this chapter in a day, you will find that you cannot incorporate all of these techniques in a single day. Start with the one that seems easiest to you and slowly build on your techniques as you become more confident. Each one of these steps is a movement in the right direction.

CHAPTER 3

OVERCOMING LIMITING BELIEFS

We all have our problem areas; beliefs that we have that dictate what goals we set and what we try to do in our lives. Even if you do not realize it, it is very likely that you have an ingrained belief system that controls what you do with your life. In most cases, these place restrictions on you and limit your ability to grow to your full potential. When you are a spy, overcoming these beliefs is critical. Even the slightest doubt in yourself or the slightest hint of uncertainty can make doing your job nearly impossible. This is especially true since you do not always know what is coming, just like when you are dealing with life.

One of the hardest beliefs I have had to overcome in my professional work was convincing myself that I could handle the art of interrogation. In my stint with the FBI, I only had the displeasure of interrogating a suspect on a few occasions and the first was tough. I was working late when one of my coworkers (we will call him Frank) needed help interrogating a guy who had performed multiple high level credit card fraud violations across the state. Frank's partner had gone out on a lunch break (it was 11pm and closer to dinner time for everyone else but these fella's worked all night) regardless he was gone for a while. Later, we learned that he got held up on a robbery call.

In the days when I was working my desk job, I was not the most extroverted person and I often went out of my way to avoid confrontation. For instance, as I have mentioned previously I ended up taking on extra jobs sometimes just because I had a hard time saying "No". This was probably the reason I felt obligated to help when Frank asked me, even though I literally had zero experience interrogating suspects. I pointed this out to Frank as we walked down to the interrogation room, where the suspect had already been waiting for about 3 hours. I was familiar with this psychological tactic, the time alone made the criminal think, wore them down.

Frank said we would have to break him. With my lack of experience, Frank decided to go first. He told me I could observe for a while and then come in when he gave me the signal, a slight hand gesture. It would be my job to keep the guy talking while Frank walked out of the room to "compose" himself, another interrogation technique. This one was of the good cop/bad cop sort.

Frank gave the signal. I took a deep breath and walked into the room. Upon me entering the room, he said, "I suppose you're down here to tell me to back off, right?"

"C'mon, man, you don't want to destroy the guy. Give it a rest." I calmly stated.

"I'm just getting started!" Frank yelled at the guy in the chair, as he slammed his fists on the table before he stormed out of the room.

"How are you doing man?" I asked him. I pretended to take a minute to look over his file, even though Frank had already briefed me. I let out a low whistle.

"They got you good man. Did they offer you a deal yet or are you trying to take this to trial?"

We talked for a few minutes. I built a decent rapport with the guy whilst subtly intimating that we had enough evidence to put him away for a while (even though the paper trail we had on this guy was flimsy at best) and that he should take a plea deal to shorten his sentence. I had initially thought that I wouldn't be able to interrogate him, but I did pretty well playing the good cop part. Frank came back in after about five minutes and went in for the kill. He got the guy to confess in no time at all.

For me, it turns out I did pretty well on my first attempt at this. Even though I had never performed an official interrogation before as I didn't think I'd be any good at it in the slightest. I wasn't good with confrontations and interactions with people in my early years, which is why I hid behind a desk. But I was incredibly grateful for my first interrogation, because it gave me that boost of confidence I needed to know I would be good in the field. I couldn't have possibly foreseen my future with the CIA, but I at least knew that I was no longer limited by my ability to interact with people in confrontational situations. It prepared me a great deal for what was to come.

Why You Need to Overcome Limiting Beliefs

While overcoming limiting beliefs is essential to working as a spy, it is also a skill that you should perfect for day to day life. When you have limiting beliefs, they hold you back big time. Have you ever avoided doing something because you didn't think you would be any good at it? Your lack of confidence in yourself is what leads you to shy away from new opportunities and different experiences. The major problem with this is that we get stuck in a comfort zone. While a comfort zone is a nice place to be, you will find that you are stuck after time goes by. This is because your limiting beliefs prevent you from moving forward and reaching your maximum potential. After all, how can you set the bar higher for yourself when you are afraid to reach that high? The rest of this chapter will teach you how to stop your limiting beliefs from controlling your life, step by step.

Step 1: Isolate the Belief that is Limiting You

Before you can address the belief affecting your life, you have to find out what it is. Often, our limiting beliefs are embedded deeply in the mind and we may not even realize that they are controlling what we do (and what we do not do) in our lives.

I want you to stop for a moment and think about the last time you decided to do something (or not to do something). Now, consider why you made the choice. For example, imagine you were invited out to do something with your coworkers. You said no and made up some excuse about needing to do work or just being too exhausted to go out. Did you really have to work or were you avoiding them because of an underlying belief? Discovering your underlying belief will require some digging, but it is possible. In many cases where social situations are avoided, the underlying belief could be something like "I am not good at interacting with people" or "They will not like me once they know me". Once you have isolated whatever belief is plaguing you, it is time to move on to the next step.

Step 2: Figure out Where the Belief Comes From

Did you know that we can have a single conversation with someone and it can change our entire outlook on life? It takes only one teacher to belittle you and tell you that you are not good in math or science and that can affect your future career choices. Maybe instead of becoming an engineer and designing life-changing products you end up working as a journalist, limiting the talent and good you could provide to the world. Think about the underlying belief that you identified in the first step. Think back to when you first heard that belief and how many times you heard it before you believed it. When you know where the belief came from, you are ready to start eliminating it from your mind.

I am going to return to the story I told in the beginning of this chapter. I believed that I was incapable of confronting someone because I may screw it up in some way. It took quite a bit of digging on my part, but I related this fear all the way back to 7th grade. There was a kid in the grade above me who made it a point to trip me in the hallway, prank me, typical middle school bully stuff. One day, I was tired of it. My father asked me about what was going on. When I told him, he advised me to stand up for myself. To take a few deep breaths, stand tall, and refuse to put up with it. I wasn't totally sure what that meant in terms of an action plan but it sounded sensible.

I entertained this behavior from this annoying kid for another two weeks or so, working up the courage to carry out my father's advice. Even with my preparation (of course I wasn't a psychology buff back in those days and I knew nothing about gaining confidence), I could not foresee how poorly the encounter would go. I did stand up to him. But then he decided to push me and then I punched him and it led to my first suspension of my school career. My parents at least understood the situation, it was kind of their advice, but I was jumpy ever since. Even though the bully left me alone from that point onward, I was still somewhat timid and afraid of confrontations after that. That small incident may have seemed insignificant to someone else, but it made a telling impact on me and I only realized quite how much so when I thought it through later in life.

My fear of confrontation was later enforced in my junior year of high school. I had been dating a girl who was a freshman; the age difference didn't seem like much to us. I graduated to a senior before she would finally introduce me to her parents. I learned why too, they were incredibly strict. Her father interrogated me like I had never seen before. I do not even grill suspects to the extreme that this man went with me. Panic set in and I froze up. When I answered, I stuttered and nothing was coming out right. While my girlfriend and I tried to sneak around for a while, it eventually lost its appeal and we both moved on to other things.

Step 3: Realize the Belief for What it is- A Belief and Not Facts

If you have completed the steps above, then you are probably already starting to realize that the thoughts ingrained into your mind are not necessarily the truth. You may also have started to realize all of the times that these beliefs limited your abilities or held you back. It is very likely that you have held onto this belief for so long because you thought it to be true. The first step in undoing your false beliefs and the results they bring is realizing that the beliefs are just that, a state of mind. There are no facts behind them, they are simply perceptions you made and meanings you attributed to things as a child (for the most part) and you only believe the lie today because it has been ingrained into your brain for so long.

As you think, allow yourself to feel emotions. You may be sad or even angry at the opportunities that you have missed out on because you were afraid. I myself find myself angry at the extreme limits that I placed on my career in the first decade of my work, because I did not think I was good enough to move up and handle confrontations with criminals. I lacked confidence in myself, and my career suffered.

Once you have considered the limiting belief and exactly how it has affected you throughout your life, accept that you are not perfect. You too are capable of making mistakes, as am I, as is every person that you come across in your life. Nobody is perfect and part of this imperfection sometimes comes down to the way that we think and how it affects our lives. Once you have accepted that you are not perfect, be ready to change. Open your mind by being willing to learn and make the changes necessary to overcome your limiting beliefs and reach for all of the things that you deserve and can achieve in life.

Step 4: Empower Yourself with New Beliefs

The best way to eliminate a negative belief is to replace it with a better, more positive one. A belief which actually serves you, instead of holding you back. This can sometimes be tricky as the things that really hold people back are usually subconscious feelings of low self worth and that they are undeserving of material wealth, good relationships, a successful career or whatever it maybe. These underlining beliefs can be harder to spot and in turn replace as they are often below the surface and once again came from childhood so have been there for a long time. But they are well worth identifying if you can. A technique that worked for me was releasing that the people who affected me in the examples above were just human beings trying to work life out, as I was. I attributed meanings to their actions in a negative way towards me when there was really no meaning at all. Taking yourself back to these moments and realizing this for yourself can produce a profound shift in how you now view them and ultimately how you now view yourself.

For more surface level beliefs, it's a good idea to choose ones which are realistic. If you honestly do not have a skill, convincing yourself that you do have it can lead to disappointment and even disaster in the future. Imagine, for example, that you have stayed in a comfortable position at work, quiet about your ideas, because you are terrified of needing to give a presentation. This lack of self-confidence has limited you in your career.

To form an empowering belief, you do not just want to negate what you believed before. Additionally, you do not want to set the bar too high for yourself. Do not think that you can empower yourself with the belief that you ARE an incredible public speaker and expect to nail it, especially if you do not take the time to properly prepare. Instead, empower yourself with the belief that you CAN learn to be a good public speaker. Believe that you have the capability and the confidence to learn how to speak in front of any crowd, especially with the right techniques.

Another trick to finding the right empowering beliefs is to imagine a future once you develop the skill that you can learn. Think about what skills you may learn as a result of the belief and that it has the potential to affect your future in such a positive way. You will then find it easier to bring into your reality.

Step 5: Act Out Your New Belief

Once you have chosen an empowering belief, take a moment to consider how someone that had this belief would act. Imagine how they would walk as they go about their day and how they would speak to and interact with people. Then, be an actor. Act as if your newfound belief is part of your life.

Eventually, your mind will not be able to tell when you are acting and when you are not. This works in the same way that traditional brainwashing works, consistent behaviors lead to learning the behaviors. Something as simple as changing the way that you talk, speaking and making eye contact, and standing with better posture can help you learn to be more confident.

Step 6: Set Goals and Achieve Success

The best way to instill a new belief is to provide evidence of your success. Repeated evidence of doing well in something will make you feel more confident in that area. In turn, the evidence will allow the new belief to overpower and take president over the old belief.

In most cases, you are going to want to start small with your goals. Imagine that you are afraid of speaking to people you don't know, making you believe it is impossible to speak with them. This has affected your social life and people like clerks and cashiers sometimes think you are rude. Start with politeness as you talk to strangers, simply remembering to hold doors and say "after you" or thanking people. Work your way up to small talk, talking about sports or the weather with cashiers, clerks, and even people on the elevator. Eventually, allow yourself to go out to a comedy club or other popular spot and talk to strangers.

It is important to celebrate your success as you complete each of your goals. Remember that every time you do something new, it can never be undone. This was a success and nothing can refute that new success. Continue building evidence of your new beliefs until it is ingrained in your mind and reflected in all that you do. If you find that you have other limiting beliefs holding you back, eliminate these as well. Continue to change your limiting beliefs until your confidence in yourself skyrockets and you will naturally start to thrive and grow.

Hopefully the above chapters have given you an overview of the importance in developing an overarching and solid general self-confidence and how you should go about starting to cultivate this into your everyday life. Having steadfast self-confidence in your skills and abilities really does underpin everything you will do in life and is the basis for all future success. This is why I started here.

The following section (part 2) contains chapters that will focus more directly on situational self-confidence techniques. For those specific meetings and events you can prepare for in advance. This is really where my specialty lies.

PART 2

PREPARING FOR IMPORTANT OCCASIONS- DATES, INTERVIEWS, MEETINGS AND MORE

CHAPTER 4

DOING YOUR HOMEWORK

You cannot expect to jump into a situation and get the most out of it unless you have done your homework beforehand. This chapter will teach you what you should know before you go on that date; take that important interview, or sit down for that critical business meeting. Working as a spy, doing your homework is obviously essential to an operations success. But it's also something that applies to civilian life, for those critical encounters you know you need to take full advantage of, since being prepared allows you a much higher level of confidence going into that opportunity. This chapter will teach you just that, i.e. everything you need to know to win in any situation.

Tip #1: Recce the Location

Exploring a new area can be mentally exhausting, especially once you have to find somewhere to park, find the door, and then find the area where your meeting/interview/date is. My advice is always head over to the location a week in advance & scope out the area as much as you can before the actual day of your meeting. Go to the lobby of the building or sit down at the restaurant and have a coffee, familiarizing yourself with the location. Identify exactly what floor and exactly what office or unit you need to be at. On the day of your event, you will not have to spend any time trying to figure out where you need to be, how to navigate the different areas of the building, where the elevators are positioned etc allowing you to arrive with your mind fully focused. This may seem trivial, but I assure you, the less mental energy you expend on this stuff the better.

When I think back to the situation where I needed to place the surveillance equipment around the warehouse, it was a tricky one since their operations didn't really allow me to go in and survey the area before my arriving on the day. Knowing the area, like always, was essential to my mission since an air conditioning expert would obviously know his way around the building.

I was fortunate enough to obtain schematics of the building. This was not as optimal as going to the physical location and scoping it out would have been, but it would have to do for my particular situation. I studied the floor plan, marking key areas where I would need to hide the surveillance equipment. On the day of the operation I wasn't disorientated in the slightest and I met the objective with flying colors. I found myself calmer and less flustered, which allowed me to think clearly when the guys started asking me questions. This proved critical to my success.

Tip #2: Come Prepared (But Don't Over Think It)

Regardless of what you are preparing for, do what research you can to ensure it will be a success. If you have competitors, learn what you can about them. If you are interviewing for a job, learn about the company attitude and consider what type of personality they will respond positively to. If you are going on a date, spend time on your date's social media accounts (no stalking), learning a little about what they like so you can think of conversation topics. Learn everything about what you need from all angles and once you have the intelligence, use it to your advantage. There's no trick here, just hard work and a little research.

As a spy, most of the work that I did was based on psychological warfare. For interrogation, information extraction, or other reasons, learning about the individual and subsequently using psychological techniques to get what was needed was paramount. You had to research your mark and learn all you could, finding out how they will respond to various personality traits & behavioral patterns. Then adapt your own behavior accordingly to optimally get the most out of them. I have been undercover for months at a time, sometimes becoming so enveloped in the role I was playing that it's often gets difficult to discern the cover story from the real you. It's a tough game because whatever personality you use, you have to remain consistent. You step into the shoes of your personality and remain there for hours, sometimes even days at a time.

I'm not saying that you have to go this far, or everyday encounters require this level of commitment. But some thorough research and due diligence on your interviewer before sitting that critical meeting is always time well spent.

At the same time, you should realize there is a difference between being prepared and obsessing/over thinking about something. You should learn all that you can about what you are going into, but you do not want to get yourself too worked up. Come prepared, but do not allow it to consume your thought so much that you become anxious. Over thinking too much will actually be counterproductive to confidence, so make sure to stop and relax if you find yourself obsessing.

Tip #3: 'Act as If' Principle

Have you ever entered a situation where you didn't know what you would do? You may have been incredibly nervous, even sweating or feeling like you had to throw up. This isn't uncommon. After all, how can you prepare adequately if you don't know what to expect?

You will find the key to success in this area is to act confident. This is the 'fake it 'til you make it' principle or 'act as if' method. Basically, if you act confident and sure of yourself, you will trick yourself into becoming confident and sure of yourself. This is true regardless of what task you are facing. Even if you have not had that specific experience, tell yourself you had similar experiences and you know how to act. If you find that you have no experience in the area, imagine that you are an actor. Do and say the things that you believe someone who was experienced and confident would do and say.

You will want to start this process as soon as you can, well before the date of your occasion if you can. Your mind will start to adopt these actions as being second nature. It starts to change your physiology as you do it.

Did I start sweating when those warehouse guys started to ask me probing questions? A little, but nothing I couldn't deal with. I stayed cool and calm as I answered their questions and then I continued on my way. I contribute my success mostly to this principle and the fact that I had done plenty of research beforehand of course.

Tip #4: Learn the Lingo

Imagine you want to be a lawyer and that you were casually talking to an experienced one as they started to tell a joke but filled it with confusing vocabulary, words that are used specifically in law cases. Chances are, you wouldn't understand the joke, and your chance of being taken seriously would be slim.

Learning the common vocabulary is always something I did before approaching anybody with any level of importance or any gatekeeper to what I needed to achieve. People in every field of work/life will use certain terminology which if you do not know, will highlight you as an amateur and pretty quickly at that. This is bad news if you are trying to get a leg up in that interview. Try to attain at least a base level of competence here by reading around the subject as much as possible. Read the articles and blogs your future colleagues/peers would read as they will talk in the vocabulary most common to them in those publications.

During my first few months in the CIA, I was involved in a number of operations on US soil to warm me up for more difficult foreign ops. This included being shipped to the outer parts of the Washington D.C. area, in a pretty rough neighborhood. The idea was that I would go undercover in a local street gang dealing in high end stolen cars. Think of the movie "Gone in 60 Seconds" but way less glamorous.

Let me tell you, at first glance, I definitely don't look like I belong in a professional car stealing outfit. I am of fairly average height. I'm a muscular build, but not too heavily set. I have a five o'clock shadow most of the day, plain brown hair. Oh, and I wear glasses, at least I did when I was working the desk. I don't have any special kind of look; I'm just your average looking guy. My objective was to infiltrate the gang, finding out what I could about their operation. I have to admit that when I put on the clothes I was supposed to wear, I felt ridiculous. They had suited me in a tracksuit and a baggy white t-shirt. I wore contacts for this one, since glasses would be hard to keep on if I ended up in any high speed chases. This proved to be a good idea.

In the end getting a foot in the door with these guys wasn't that difficult as I was easily able to hotwire a car and steal it as my induction. It was more the lingo they spoke and vocabulary they used that would give me away.

The guys in charge of the operation made sure I looked the part, but I also had to act the part. A lot of this was learning the lingo. Gang members at this level were incredibly cautious of new people and the slightest slip in my personality could mean blowing my cover. I spent weeks researching top end car specs, even pulling a few guys in off the nearby streets that owed me favors, to make sure I really spoke their language.

Tip #5: Dress the Part

How confident would you feel if you spent a business meeting adjusting your shirt, because it didn't fit your body well? How clearly could you think with shoes pinching your toes? Like acting the part, dressing the part will help you feel confident and sure of yourself as you go about your business. As you dress, think about how other people would dress. If you have a meeting with a specific company or are interviewing, choose a position-appropriate outfit.

You should also consider how you want people to perceive you. Whether you admit it or not, your mind subconsciously judges people on the way that they are dressed. The way you act upon this initial perception is up to you, but it's very difficultly discount this first impression. If you dress in well-fitting clothes that are clean, you will come across as someone who has their life together.

When I was being dressed for the role of a gang member, I wanted to be perceived as someone from the streets, but also someone that could be respected. This is the reason that the guys chose a tracksuit over baggy or dirty clothing. I looked like someone who could be respected, but I still gave off the streets attitude and personality.

Something to remember as you choose your clothes though is to stay comfortable. You will not be able to give your meeting or date the attention it needs if you cannot focus because your clothes aren't comfortable. Choose clothes, shoes, and accessories that fit well and that are appropriate for how you want people to perceive you. Pick out your clothes at least a couple days before, in case you find that something doesn't fit well or it needs cleaned before your occasion.

Whilst your outward facing image/appearance to the world isn't what you'll derive the majority of your self-confidence from, being well dressed with clothes that fit will feed into the positive confidence feedback loops you are continually nurturing.

If you follow these 5 tips for preparing for the day of an important meeting, date, interview, or any other important occasion where you need to excel, you will walk in feeling naturally more confident. Adding these things in with your confidence-building skills from the last chapter will help you give off an unshakeable air of confidence.

CHAPTER 5

POSITIVE VISUALIZATION FOR SUCCESS

Visualization is something that has been around for centuries. It was even described by Aristotle more than 2,000 years ago. He described positive visualization as finding a clear goal, having the means to reach your goal, and then visualizing your means reaching the end goal. This chapter will teach you how to do each step.

How Positive Visualization Works to Improve Confidence

It is important that you do not confuse the technique discussed here with the "think it and you can achieve it" technique from many leading self-help authors. The objective of this kind of positive visualization, instead, is to help improve your performance by increasing your confidence.

Did you know that the mind can't distinguish between things that you actually experience and stories that you play in your mind? This is especially true at the subconscious level, which is responsible for a lot of the things that we feel. Numerous studies have shown that the physiological result is the same, regardless of if you are running the scenario through your head or actually experiencing it. If you don't want to take my word for it, here is some of the science behind it.

A study by Guang Yue at the Cleveland Clinic Foundation of Ohio tested increase in muscle mass in people who did virtual workouts and people who went to the gym every day. The people who virtually exercised had a 13.5% improvement in muscle mass while the group who actually went to the gym saw a 30% increase. The interesting thing was that Yue and his associates tested the group who mentally trained three months after the study, finding that they retained their muscle mass even without further training.

In another study, the brain patterns of weightlifters were studied. It was found that imagining the act of weightlifting lit up the same pattern of neurons in the brain that lifting hundreds of pounds does.

This type of visualization is also highly popular in sports and athletic events. The Soviets have cited the use of this technique since the 1970s for giving athletes an edge in sports competitions. Athletes like Muhammad Ali and Tiger Woods have also credited much of their success to visualization techniques.

So, what does this collection of evidence mean for you? All of the studies, as well as the performance of athletes, actors, and more, have benefited from positive visualization. The reason is in the mind-body connection. The evidence, as you can see, points to the fact that the subconscious mind cannot differ between visualization and actually doing an activity. That means that when you visualize your meeting, date, or other event from beginning to end, it lights up the same neuron path in the brain as if you were actually doing the activity. As you visualize yourself completing the task, you become more familiar with it. Since your mind feels as if you have done the activity/completed the meeting already, you will be more confident that you can complete it.

Step 1: Have a Clear Objective

You have to have a destination before you can decide on the route you must take to get there. To form a successful visualization, first, consider your end goal. Think about what you want to accomplish. Imagine every aspect of your success. Think about the clothes you are wearing, how you feel in the moment, even how success sounds. Use as many senses as you can as you consider your goal, going as deeply in detail as you can. Check out the following example.

Imagine that you are preparing for a presentation for big executives. Your objective is to give a presentation and convince the executives to buy your software product. Picture what you are wearing as you give the last line of your presentation. The executive at the head of the table stands, saying, "Let's set this up" and reaching out to shake your hand. Feel the warmth of happiness in your cheeks and the way his hand feels in yours as you seal the deal. Imagine the lift around the corners of your mouth and the warm glowing feeling radiating through your body.

Step 2: Being Prepared for Your Goal

Imagine someone had legal fines and had their license suspended. They visualize themselves driving in the Indy 500 everyday, even though they do not have a license, let alone a racecar to drive in. How likely do you think it is that this person would reach their objective through mental visualization alone?

If you do not have the means to meet your goal, it is unlikely that you will complete it. Visualization may give you more motivation to reach toward your goal, but it will not come true if you do not have the means to do it.

Step 3: Running Through Your Mental Playbook

You will have the best results with positive visualization if you run through it at least once a day. When you do, go to a quiet area and sit with your back tall, as a sign of confidence. Close your eyes and imagine the entire scenario, from start to finish. Use as much detail as possible, engaging your senses when you can to make the visualization more realistic. Over time, you will grow a newfound confidence in the activity you are doing. When it comes time for the event, you will be calm, composed, and confident.

Imagine once again that you have to give an important presentation to business executives about your software. You are given the notice that all of the executives have arrived. You walk down the hallway to the room where you will be giving your presentation. Then, you catch a glimpse of yourself in the mirror. You give yourself a sure look and say, "I've got this". Your clothing is neat and you are well-groomed, with a cool and calm composure. In your right hand, you are holding the folder with the business contracts- already prepared for your success. In your left hand, you feel the buttons of the remote that will help you go through your PowerPoint presentation that has already been set up, double-checked for accuracy.

You reach with your left hand and reach for the metal doorknob, noticing how cool it feels in your palm. You turn it easily and confidently stride into the room, easily switching your folder from the right hand to the left. You shake hands with the two business executives at the head of the table and give a quick nod to everyone else. Then, you go through your presentation flawlessly. All of your PowerPoint slides are in order and every word that you say is clear and concise.

Now, you have reached the point of your objective. Once again, imagine your success as you deliver the last line of your presentation and the joy as you close the deal.

When used the right way, positive visualization can help build your confidence and lead you toward success, even in situations that you have never been in before. You will find that the keys to doing this is giving it your full focus and ensuring that you have all of the things you need to complete your goal. You will also need an incredibly vivid picture of your success. This will help drive you and keep you motivated in pursuing your goal. It will also increase your confidence, because your mind will believe that you have already done the situations you have played in your mind.

Running positive visualization techniques and mental playbooks similar to the ones stated above were critical during my time in the CIA. We often only got one shot at something so doing everything I could to ensure I was mentally ready was key. Envisaging the interactions going smoothly again and again in your mind, feed's into those positive confidence feedback loops once more.

CHAPTER 6

TIPS FOR THE DAY OF THE EVENT

Doing your homework and the positive visualization techniques described in the previous chapters can really help in terms of preparing for your event within the days leading up to it. Those techniques will build confidence in what you have to do, as well as allow you to be prepared with the knowledge and know-how to succeed on the day of your meeting, presentation, or date. Even though you are incredibly well prepared, the following tips will help you that one step further by giving you an edge on the day of the event itself.

#1: Sleep Well

This one is fairly obvious, but on the night prior to your big appointment, make sure that you get plenty of sleep. On average, adults need between 7 and 8 hours of sleep each night to operate optimally. You know what your body needs, so adjust this to the amount of sleep that you need to be refreshed. On the day of your interview, do your positive visualization routine in the morning.

You may also want to exercise if you regularly do, to keep yourself feeling fresh and alert. Finally, eat a healthy breakfast with brain-healthy foods the morning of your event. Include things like Omega-3s for healthy brain function to stay focused and low glycemtic index whole grains to allow for gradual and slow release of energy throughout the day.

As a spy, every day is an important appointment. This is the reason that I stress having a regular healthy regimen that you follow. It allows you to start every day off the right way and also gives you consistency that will help build on your confidence, because you are ready to start each day well.

#2: Give Yourself Time

Have you ever been late for something and felt your heart racing, wondering if you were going to make it on time or if you were going to miss your appointment, be reprimanded by your boss, or face other consequences? Being late is never a good thing, because it shows ill preparation. You may also find yourself making mistakes like forgetting to put on deodorant or forgetting to brush your hair as you rush to get ready. Not a good look.

Start by laying out your clothes the night before, making sure that everything is easy to locate in the morning. Also keep your wallet, car keys, and materials that you may need for your occasion together, so you do not forget anything. Wake up early, allowing yourself plenty of time to prepare. Then, leave your house at least 30 minutes early to avoid rushing. You do not want to arrive flustered or even worse, sweaty because you had to run to make it on time.

#3: Make a Great First Impression

From the moment someone first sees you, their mind will start to assess you and make judgments. This is why it is important to dress well, smell good, and be well-groomed whenever you have an important presentation, date, or meeting. In addition to all of these things, you want to take the steps to build a great rapport and give off an air of confidence, letting everyone know that you are sure of yourself. As you greet everyone, address him or her by name. You should also practice good, strong handshakes and making eye contact with people. These are all habits that confident people use and it will show that you are a strong person who is sure of themselves. It will put everybody at ease.

#4: Exist in the Moment (Situational Awareness)

You cannot give an amazing presentation nor have a great date if you are constantly wondering how it is going to end or wondering what the other party is thinking. When you are involved in something, it is important that you give it your entire focus. Do your best to exist in the moment, noticing the things around you and paying close attention to the body language of other people, as well as your own.

While you should exist in the moment, it's also a good idea to think just one or two steps ahead. Being prepared for questions you may be asked or making small talk will prepare you for this, pay close attention to what is happening so you can adjust your tone if necessary. Thinking ahead a few seconds into the future if you are anticipating questions or another response is a wise tactic if it doesn't take you out of the present moment. However, do not think so far ahead that you are worrying about what is going to happen instead of focusing on the task at hand.

As a spy, you have to learn to both exist in the moment and think ahead. The importance of being able to pick up on crucial cues and being able to react to the situation goes without saying. This has a lot to do with reading the people around you, paying close attention to their body language and how they are reacting to what you have to say. Information you cannot fully absorb if you are not intensely present.

#5: Learn the Art of Small Talk

Small talk is an incredibly useful habit. Basically, talk to everyone! If you are going to a date, meeting, or other important occasion, start by talking to the 'peripheral' people in and around the building. This is especially useful if you are naturally more introverted. Some of the people you may talk to include door staff, secretaries, waiters, and anyone else you encounter leading up to the event.

The benefits to doing this are twofold. The first is that it loosens you up and gets you ready to converse. This is especially beneficial if you have approach anxiety, because it gets you in the rhythm of interacting with people. The second benefit of small talk is that you might pick up on some important nugget of information that you wouldn't have otherwise gotten. This might be something small that can help you interact with the person or organization you are about to meet with. If a secretary tells you that the guy you are waiting for is late due to dropping his boy off at soccer practice, slip into your conversion with him how you love watching your own kids play soccer!

This is something that is incredibly useful when you are a spy, particularly the bit about picking up interesting tidbits of information. When you are collecting intelligence on a person or organization, talking to people who may know of them was mandatory. I remember one time that I was trying to speak with a CEO of a big business I was gathering intelligence on. He was less than willing to talk to me. When I had asked to speak to him, his secretary said he had already left. I tried my luck with various people around the building, even the attendant of the parking garage. He was quite puzzled when he pointed out the CEO's parking spot, which was filled with his car. I waited him out and eventually got to do my questioning.

#6: Practice Story Telling

The ability to tell a good story can come in handy in a number of situations. You can use it to allude to a presentation, break the ice for a business meeting or date, or answer a question in an interview. I've had many situations in both my professional and civilian life where this has come in handy. Usually, it was used as a stall if my cover was about to be compromised. If things were going bad, a few canned anecdotes would often give you enough room to maneuver out of situation or even an extraction team time to step in if things really got hairy.

The ability to be a good story teller is also a very interesting and attractive personality trait in of itself. It can smooth the tension in many situations. Do your best to practice telling a few stories that you can fall back on in different situations that you may find yourself in. It may help you when you need to apply the following tactic.

#7: Always Have an Exit Strategy

Sometimes, you just need to get out of a situation. Whether you need to escape a bad date or step out of a presentation for a moment to compose yourself, always have a way to leave but maintain good etiquette. Politely excuse yourself to find a drink of water or have a friend waiting for your SOS text. Think of a way that you can leave without being rude, just in case you need it.

I was once working a case on the Russian mafia in Budapest, Hungary, with real tough guys that you do not want to insult. Because of the high risk that was associated with the case, all of the proper precautions had been taken. I was wearing a miniscule microphone, located in the inner lining of one of my pockets. We were being a lot more discreet than you see in the movies, with all of those wires taped to someone's chest for surveillance. Even with my calm composure and solid back story, I could see that the mark was getting suspicious. Though he was talking to me, I could tell from his tense composure and the slight movement of his arms beneath the desk that he was about to do something. (One of the things you always find yourself doing as a spy is watching people's hands. Its hands that hold guns/knives or throw punches. If somebody hides them, it's almost always trouble). He was either about to push an alert button that signaled to his crew to take me out or pull a gun on me himself. I wasn't sure if I had offended him in some way or if he was just wary of my ruse. Regardless, I knew that I had been found out.

I had been sent in to try to sell him some unregistered guns. We needed something to nab this guy and hopefully interrogate him into giving us information on another case we were working. I had been contracted to find the whereabouts of a high profile politician's daughter. It wasn't clear if she had been kidnapped by this outfit ready to extort her family or had just gone missing and that they would have some information that could help locate her.

I had an exit strategy before I ever entered into the situation. A few of my guys were staking out the roof, ready to quickly enter through the ducts should there be any signs of trouble and I was to find the nearest exit. I had studied the building schematics beforehand to find accessible doors and windows. Before we resorted to these measures, I tried to make my exit cordially. "Alright, I can see you aren't interested. I'll be on my way," I gestured toward the door. "Hang on a minute," he said stiffly in a Moscow dialect (I could speak Russian fairly fluently at this point). When he rejected my exit, I knew things were about to go bad.

It turns out I was right about the button, two big, beefy guys came through the door into the room. I quickly made my exit out the window. It would have been slightly problematic that I was on the third floor, but the fire escape was outside waiting like I knew it would be. I quickly started to make my way down the escape. As expected, the two guys tried to follow me. They started to spray bullets, though most of them didn't even come close to hitting me. I heard a "bang" and then one of the guys screamed in pain, my team on the roof had done their job of making sure I got out of there alive.

While my exit did not end up being as classy as I had hoped it would be, I still got out of there breathing, that's what mattered, to me anyway. You are probably not a spy though, so you should aim for a little more grace than I did as you plan your exit strategy.

In most cases in everyday life it's more about having an elegant excuse you can fall back on. An urgent meeting you need to attend if things are going bad. Just make sure you plan for it ahead of time.

Hopefully the ideas and techniques within this section of the book has given you a good grounding of what's needed to cultivate high level confidence in preparation leading up to an important event as well as on the day, allowing you to operate optimally and extract the most benefit and pleasure from the experience.

The following and final section (part 3) will be the icing on the cake. For the moment's when you are truly up against it. If you have put the previous chapter's advice into practice you should already have a head start. But next you will learn how to deal with the moments that are sprung upon you; the moments even the best laid plans can't foresee which often cause swift and sudden bouts of social anxiety. This can be really debilitating to somebody who does not know how to deal with it correctly. That won't be you soon enough.

PART 3

TRICKS TO OVERRIDE SOCIAL ANXIETY IN STRESSFUL SITUATIONS

CHAPTER 7

THE OODA LOOP TO PROCESS AND RESPOND TO SURPRISING SITUATIONS

John Boyd, a United States Air Force Colonel and military strategist developed the OODA Loop. For his purpose, it was employed while developing strategic military operations. It teaches how to react in unforeseen situations. This can be very beneficial as a spy, but also in everyday life. You cannot always plan when you will run into someone or need to interact with an important business leader. When your back is against the wall and you have no time to plan, the OODA loop lets you think on your feet.

Where Can You Use the OODA Loop?

The OODA Loop was developed for the military, but it is useful in any number of situations. It is used by businesses, law enforcement, and even people in their day to day lives. The key to using the OODA loop is to process the cycles more quickly than the person you are interacting with. You can begin to expect what they may say and respond appropriately. This gives you the upper advantage in the situation.

How to Use the OODA Loop for Everyday Life

Step 1: Observe

Part one is to observe your situation. Consider the unfolding circumstances, taking note of any outside information that you may have obtained and any additional interaction with your surrounding environment. Take all of these tidbits of information and move into the next step.

Step 2: Orient

Next, you must filter the information that you have just processed. First, consider the genetic heritage or cultural traditions of the person or group you are dealing with, so you can act appropriately. Then, compare the information against any new information, your analysis of the situation unfolding around you, and your previous experiences.

Step 3: Decide

Once you have gathered everything that you could possibly know about the current situation, consider your options. Briefly consider the effects of each and decide on the one with the best possible outcome.

Step 4: Act

Once you have made a decision, you must act. You may find that you have to revert to a previous option if the situation changes, because sometimes your thought process unfolds as the environmental situation around you unfolds.

Very briefly, I am going to return to the situation where I was talking to the Russian mafia guy and my cover was blown. I had a few moments to plot my escape. I knew the fire escape was outside of the window and I also had adequate cover- the only obstacle was getting through the window. When the mob goons came in through the only other exit, the door, I knew that the window was my only option. This entire thought process took just seconds. When you are a spy, you typically only have seconds to process and make a decision in certain situations if you want to survive.

Even in your own life you may find you have to think on your feet. Practice going through the OODA cycles in your day to day life and use it when unforeseen encounters arise. You will learn to go through these cycles more quickly and as you master this technique, you may find yourself so sure of your thought and what to do that you can react to unexpected situations in the matter of seconds significantly reducing the chances you will become flustered in the first place.

CHAPTER 8

ADDITIONAL TACTICS FOR WHEN YOUR BACK IS AGAINST THE WALL

Life is unpredictable. My day to day working for the CIA certainly was. Sometimes, no matter how much you prepare you find yourself in very compromising and stressful situations. You may even find yourself faced with an encounter that is completely unexpected, when you have little time to react and your back is against the wall. When something is sprung on you and it throws you off your game. In these instances, it is critical that you have some strategies in your back pocket to downplay the nerves, self-doubt and social anxiety when they arise, and even flip the situation to give yourself the confidence boost to deal with it accordingly.

Essentially what happens when humans are put under acute stress is that the 'fight or flight' response kicks in and the sympathetic nervous system is fired up. This causes a chain reaction of cascading catecholamine hormone release from the adrenal medulla (mainly adrenalin) to ready the body to either stay and fight or flee to safety.

I won't go into the obvious evolutionary reasons for why this was once a beneficial thing for the survival of our species. Needless to say, it's a somewhat outdated physiological legacy that we could largely do without in modern day life. Not least because it greatly reduces an individual's perception and ability to think clearly when it's onset occurs. Most of what we needed to do in the field as a CIA agent was simply learning how to compensate for and downplay this inhibiting nervous system response in stressful situations. It's definitely an advantage in knowing how to do this within civilian life too. The following tips are provided to help you with just that.

#1: Keep Your Composure

One of the worst things you can do in an unexpected situation is showing the other party that you are uncomfortable. In my line of work, losing your composure is one of the quickest ways to blow your cover. In casual or business interactions, losing your composure can show nervousness, fear, and a general lack of confidence.

The key to keeping your composure is in suppressing the 'fight or flight' response I mentioned above. Anxiety can also cause this. From the second adrenaline starts pumping through your system, your ability to perceive the situation shrinks. You will lose focus and be unable to think clearly. It can also cause a rapid heartbeat, sweating, and other symptoms. You should avoid this at all costs.

If you have trouble keeping your cool, check out some of the techniques later in this chapter.

#2: Know When to Blend In

In some situations, you may find that your best option is to look calm and blend into the scene, if you aren't exactly sure what your next step is. Sometimes the best course of action you can take is to make sure you don't look out of place if you are in a tight spot. This will give you the opportunity to sit back and collect data for future interactions.

One of the trickiest moments I experienced on the job was running into a target, while I was out of character so to speak. I didn't usually spend much time in romantic relationships whilst working for the CIA for obvious reasons. However this one occasion I was out on what you might consider a second date with a girl (just grabbing a coffee in reality). Needless to say, we hadn't really discussed my job so I couldn't tell her what was going on. We were sitting down in a cafe the next city over from where I was working my current assignment.

I was really surprised when the guy I had recently been following walked into the shop. We had a rough confrontation two days prior to our meeting here, where I'd been impersonating a local postal worker for the past month or so. I was suited up for the job, bag of mail and all. He accused me of following him; I guess I was, so he was right. I assured him I wasn't and quickly made a turn and continued delivering in the opposite direction of him, putting fake mail into people's yards in an attempt to not draw any more attention to myself than

I already had. The military term for this is 'getting off the X'. It may sound simple but the premise is; movement saves lives. If somebody throws a rock at you then its best to step out of the way! I wasn't sure if he would definitely recognize me but I didn't want to take that risk, especially in a coffee shop I knew only had one exit.

So I quickly called a waitress over, asking for a menu. When she produced one, I used it to keep myself hidden from view. I proceeded to ask a string of pointless questions regarding the origin of the various coffee beans they sold. My date picked up on my weird vibe and asked when the waitress left; I told her I had just seen an old colleague I wasn't on speaking terms with. She seemed to buy it. Anyway, I sat back and observed. There wasn't a great deal to be learned here in reality, except that my guy didn't have a specific neighborhood he frequented.

#3: Practice Breathing Techniques

Deep breathing techniques can come in very handy in stressful situations. The best time to do this is just before you approach the other party or if you can step outside for a few moments. The key to deep breathing is to engage your abdominal cavity. Pull your breath in through your mouth for at least five seconds, pulling it in so that your abdomen expands. Exhale your breath through your nose, feeling your abdomen returning to its natural shape.

The reason deep breathing works is because it is the opposite type of the breathing that happens with a nervous reaction. When you have anxiety, you tend to breathe rapidly and shallow, with your breaths concentrated in your chests. When you breathe deeply, you calm your nervous system and can prevent the 'fight or flight' reaction.

#4: Be Adaptable

You will find that individual situations, as in life, are never completely cut and dry. Regardless of your preparation, things will never go entirely how you anticipated, and that's OK. My intelligence training taught me a great deal, but quite importantly that physical attributes and clever skills can get you so far, but it's often the intangibles like quickness of thought that will actually get you out of a situation.

Try to cultivate this into your thinking and practice adaptability wherever you can. Try to incorporate this into your day-to-day, when the stakes aren't high. It will be good training for when you may need it most. Similar to having a planned exit strategy (#9) knowing that you can maneuver within a situation if you need to, lends to even greater confidence in your ability to function optimally.

#5: Exercise Regularly

Ok so this isn't an 'in the moment' technique but will certainly help for when stressful situations arise if you take it onboard. When you run (or uptake any form of cardiovascular exercise), endorphins are released that give you a natural feeling of well-being. This boost can help relieve anxiety and provides a great outlet for stress relief. Regular cardiovascular and other exercise will also help to normalize your nervous system reaction and gives you better control over your breathing.

Consistent exercise, especially more long distance type endurance work has also been proven to trigger greater levels of Brain-derived Neurotrophic Factor, or BDNF, which is a protein that is simultaneously associated with creating new neurons whilst protecting existing ones in the brain. BDNF is essentially a brain regenerative agent which allows you to function more optimally in all situations.

This is something that I can attest to myself. I go for a 5k run every morning, right after a good breakfast and right before I take a shower. I'm a heavy sweater when I run; otherwise I'd probably jog to work as well. There are some occasions (not many) when I have to skip this routine due to travel. However I always find that I am edgier and tenser on these days. My performance would also be lacking; thankfully I don't spend much time in the field these days so it isn't as critical.

#6: Skip the Caffeine

Caffeine makes your heart beat faster and puts your body on high alert. If you experience frequent and/or acute anxiety attacks, then caffeine can make it worse. Skipping the caffeine can help you prepare for unexpected situations by keeping you calmer when it matters most. Caffeine is frequently found in energy drinks, and dark sodas as well as coffee. So skip them all if you can. Your body will thank you for the reduction in sugar in most cases too.

#7: Exist in the Moment

I have touched on this one in section 2 already but, it also applies here. One of the biggest reasons that people have situational anxiety is because they are thinking about what COULD possibly happen. Have you ever been talking to someone and thought "What if they think I am stupid?" or "What if they don't like me?" or "What if I say something embarrassing"? Thinking about the "what ifs" in a situation can cause extra anxiety, which you do not need when the goal is calmness and composure.

Attaining a higher state of presence will help you with just about every bit of advice I have given you within this book, perception, situational awareness, maneuverability, adaptability, all forms of decision making in fact. You are better at dealing with everything in the moment. So make sure you ground yourself often.

#8: Remember that You Are Human

People make mistakes. If you catch yourself stuttering or tripping over your words, excuse yourself. In most cases, the person or group you are talking to will understand nervousness. This is true whether you are having an interview or going on your first date. Say something like, "Excuse me, this doesn't usually happen to me but I am a little nervous". This is simple and to the point and can strangely exhibit confidence in a counterintuitive way by being frank about it. You'll probably find that someone will offer you a glass of water or a moment to compose yourself diffusing the situation.

#9: Remember Your Exit Strategies

If you have been practicing the skills in the book, then you may have already practiced one or more exit strategies. This is especially true if you are just starting out on your confidence journey. Think of a few different ways to gracefully exit a conversation, regardless of where you are. Maybe you need to use the restroom or you are late for another appointment or you need to step out for a drink. Think of something to get yourself out of there and maintain your composure as you do so.

If all else fails, then you always have this one to fall back on. This is a last resort to some degree, but it will give you some added confidence that you can fall back on it helping to negate the need to use it in the first place. It's like setting an alarm clock to wake up at a certain time but then naturally waking up just a few minutes before it goes off anyway. The act of setting it ingrained it into your subconscious to wake at that point. However if you had not, you would have probably slept right through the morning.

While it would be ideal for you to know when you are going to run into these stressful situations, be it a casual encounter or a business event, the reality is that they will often be sprung upon you. When you are not prepared, remember to keep your cool. If you find yourself getting nervous, follow the techniques in this chapter to keep your composure and when you cannot, either withdraw from the situation or use one of your exit strategies.

CONCLUSION

Well, there you have it from beginning to end: how to be confident, from the mind of a spy. Part psychology, part preparation, part knowing how to act, and part improvisation. Confidence encompasses all of these things and more. Regardless of your profession, take it from an ex-spy, having a higher level of overall confidence will have a great benefit to you in all areas of your life. From your home life to your career to your social life, a confident personality will take you places you never imagined. When you are confident, you will set the bar higher and when you set the bar higher, you will reach your highest level of potential.

Whenever you have a date, interview, business meeting, presentation, or other important event, make sure you do your homework. Learn all that you can and find out how to speak, dress, and act. Use positive visualization to help you focus on and strive for your goal. On the day of the event, use good etiquette, from strong handshakes and small talk to having a great exit strategy. Finally, practice the OODA Loop technique and situational relaxation to help you think clearly in an unexpected, stressful situation. As you do all of these things, you will naturally add to your confidence bit by bit. In times where confidence fails you, you will have a wide range of skills on hand to tackle the situation in the best way possible.

CONFIDENCE

Well, what are you waiting for? Get out in the real world and put what you have learned to the test. There is a whole world waiting for you, it's just a matter of being confident enough to seize it.

Printed in Great Britain
by Amazon